Engineering YOUR WEBSITE

by Position Builder

in easy steps and **in easy steps pocket** are imprints of
Computer Step
Southfield Road . Southam . Warwickshire CV47 0FB . England
Website: www.ineasysteps.com
Email: books@ineasysteps.com

Copyright © 2002 by Computer Step. All rights reserved. No part of this book may be reproduced or transmitted in any form or by any means, electronic or mechanical, including photocopying, recording, or by any information storage or retrieval system, without prior written permission from the publisher.

Notice of Liability

Every effort has been made to ensure that this book contains accurate and current information. However, Computer Step and the author shall not be liable for any loss or damage suffered by readers as a result of any information contained herein.

Trademarks

All trademarks are acknowledged as belonging to their respective companies.

Printed and bound in the United Kingdom

ISBN 1-84078-169-6

Acknowledgements

Written by
Ross Barnes & Matthew Evans

Edited by
Hannah Newcombe

Illustrations by
Matthew Evans

Thanks to
Neil Pick, Mike Gabb, Stephen Sandison, Louise Wiffen,
John Coles, Jason Lewis and Joanna Ransome-Wallis for all
their hard work and dedication.

ReadMe.first

This is a complete guide to SEO (Search Engine Optimisation) or Web Promotion and will benefit those with an e-business strategy looking to maximise their exposure on the Internet.

We recommend that, before any alterations are made to your website, you read this book in its entirety as hasty action can, in some cases, be damaging.

We hope that the information contained within this guide proves to be both an eye-opener and useful. Remember, in the SEO world things are always changing so keep your eyes peeled and your ear to the ground.

Contents

1. Introduction — 1
What is a Search Engine? — 2
What is a Directory? — 3
What is Search Engine Optimisation? — 3
How will it Benefit Me? — 3
What do I Need to Start? — 4

2. Keywords — 5
The Importance of Keywords — 5
Defining your Market — 6
Keyword Selection — 6
    Wordtracker — 7
Stop and Filter Words — 9
Keyword Phrases — 9
Competitor Analysis — 12
Define Weighting — 13
Keyword Density — 14
Conclusion — 14

3. Design Optimisation — 15
The Importance of Good Design — 15
Title — 16

Meta Tags	17
Body Content	21
Images	22
Links	23
Tables	23
Text Formatting	24
Frames	25
Flash	28
Conclusion	28

4. Doorways and Gateways — 29

What are Doorways?	29
What are Gateways?	30
The Importance of Doorways and Gateways	31
Designing a Doorway Page	31
Designing a Gateway Page	32
Link Popularity	33

5. Tips and Tricks — 35

Planning for each Search Engine	35
The Invisible Pixel	36
Absolute Links	37
Hidden Text	37
Hidden Links	38
ASCII	39
Keywords Working Harder	40
Comment Tags	40
Cascading Style Sheets (CSS)	41

6. Advanced Techniques — 43

JavaScript Redirection	44
Cloaking	45
Robot Handling	46
Presto Chango	48
Spamming	49
Hidden Form Fields	50

7. The Search Engines — 51

Who Indexes What?	61
Crawling	61
Indexing	63
Ranking	65
Spam	66

8. Submission Tips — 69

Final Check	69
Manual Submission	69
How to Submit your Website	70
AltaVista	70
All The Web	72
Google	73
Yahoo	74
HotBot	75
Open Directory	76
LookSmart	78
Excite	79
Lycos	81

Submission Times	82
Indexing Times	82
Search Engines	82
Directories	86
Human Contact	87
Positiontech	88

9. Promotional Methods — 89

Paid Solutions	89
Paid Inclusion	90
Paid Placement	92
Pay-per-Click	97
Link Farms	101
Link Exchange	101

10. Conclusion — 103

Your Work's Not Over Yet!	103
Monitoring and Maintaining Your Position	104
Java Code	106
Dynamically Generated Pages	106

Glossary — 107

Index — 117

1

Introduction

The world of Internet marketing is forming and changing at a rapid pace. Thousands of companies now sell through the web, and competition for new customers is fierce. If you are considering starting a business online, or you already have a website, you will probably have many questions and concerns. You might be worried about your chances of success, especially considering the number of online businesses similar to your own. You may be wondering how to attract customers to your site, how to stay ahead of your competitors, or how the search engines work. If so, then this guide is for you! We will take you step by step through the process of search engine optimisation. This chapter explains what this is, as well as some of the other basic expressions that will appear again and again throughout this guide.

What is a Search Engine?

A search engine is a computer-operated database of web pages. Today there are hundreds of search engines on the web, but only a small number of them (about 15) monopolise the market, attracting roughly 85% of all Internet users.

If you are looking for a particular product or service on the Internet, you will probably do a search enquiry, by typing in one or two words (referred to as "keywords") that describe what you are looking for. You then submit these to a search engine, which sends out a "spider" (also called a "robot"). This is a program that searches for sites that are relevant to your keywords. The search engine then presents you with a results list of all the sites containing the keywords you typed in. This list can sometimes be tens or even hundreds of pages long, depending on the popularity of the keywords.

Another of the spider's jobs is to place sites into relevant positions when they are first submitted to a search engine. It does this by scanning through the HTML code of the site. The process of being added to a search engine or directory is called indexing. The position where the spider places the site depends upon a number of factors – these will be discussed in detail throughout this guide.

Examples of popular search engines are Lycos, AltaVista and AOL.

What is a Directory?

A directory is a human-run search engine. When you submit your website to a directory, an editor will look at it and decide which category it should be placed into. For example, a website about plant pots would be placed under "gardening". In this sense a directory is similar to the Yellow Pages, whereas a search engine is more like a telephone directory. The most popular directory is Yahoo, although there are many others, such as LookSmart and Open Directory.

What is Search Engine Optimisation?

Search Engine Optimisation (commonly known as SEO) refers to the techniques that are used to give a website maximum exposure to its potential customers. This is achieved by making the changes necessary to improve the site's position in search engine listings. This guide will take you step by step through the ways in which you can optimise your own website. A common misconception is that SEO is to do with web page design; in fact it is quite different to this. In a nutshell, web page design will make your site visually appealing to people when they find it, but SEO will *enable* them to find it!

How will it Benefit Me?

Quite simply, Search Engine Optimisation will bring more visitors to your website, which in turn means more potential customers and greater financial success for your business. It is worth taking the time to optimise your website. In the same way that you would not submit your website to the search engines without making sure that it looks good, you should not submit it until it is fully optimised. Both of these factors are equally important.

There is no point in having a stunningly attractive website that no one ever finds, *or* in having an unpleasant looking site that is right at the top of search engine listings.

What do I Need to Start?

In order to be able to optimise your website you will need the following:

- A computer and a website!

- A basic knowledge of web design

- A basic knowledge of HTML

- A reasonably good grasp of the English language

Now that we have covered the basic terms, we will move on to look at keywords in Chapter 2, and how to use them to your best advantage.

2

Keywords

The Importance of Keywords

Let's suppose that a potential customer is browsing on the Internet and that they happen to be looking for exactly the same product or service that your company offers. Unless they already know the address of the site they want, they will probably type in one or two keywords and the search engine will come up with a list of relevant sites. The first sites on this list will undoubtedly attract the most attention. If your site is not listed highly, you are likely to be losing many potential customers to those that are. It is important that your keywords accurately describe what your site is all about and that they relate to your potential customers, so that your site will attract the right kind of people.

Defining your Market

Think of three or four words that best describe your online business. Remember, these are the kinds of words which your potential customers will need to type in to find your website. It may help to ask an outsider to describe your company in a few words; this will give you an idea of the keywords people may use to find your site.

There are many other online companies offering the same service or product as you. It is important for you to select your keywords carefully.

Keyword Selection

By now you should have an idea of the kind of keywords your competitors are using, as well as the ones you need to use. Choosing your keywords is potentially the most crucial step in your online marketing strategy. There is little point in being at the top of a search enquiry list for a keyword which no one ever uses; this would be about as much use as having a billboard down a mine! Ideally, you need to find a keyword which is both an uncompetitive phrase (rarely used by other companies) and which is also frequently searched for by many people. This may seem impossible, given the vast number of online businesses similar to your own. Luckily, the Internet has provided us with tools to find out exactly which words are worth using and which are not.

Wordtracker

Wordtracker (www.position-builder/wordtracker) helps you find all keyword combinations that bear any relation to your business or service – many of which you might never have considered. It compiles a database of terms that people search for. You enter some keywords, and it tells you how often people search for them, and also tells you how many competing sites use those keywords. You'll find out how popular these keywords *really* are. You need related keywords to take advantage of other keywords that mean the same thing. You'll end up with a lot more traffic.

What will I get if I enter GOLF? Three hundred related words per search…

tee time	tiger woods
pga	us open
golf vacation	british open
green	putter
golf clubs	fairway
golfer	iron

Once you have found all the words that relate to your business, you can check these words in the popularity database. Click on golf to receive up to 500 keywords for each search…

Count*	Keyword
1902	golf
810	golf clubs
351	golf equipment
320	golf courses
205	used golf clubs

*Number of times the word has appeared in the database

Capitalise on misspellings:

Keyword
golf clugs
golf glubs
golf equiptment
golf eqipment

This is great for finding niches. No one on the net really targets misspellings. How can they? They don't know what they are.

Now you have an understanding of the keywords people will be using to find a site like yours. Pick four or five of the words you have come up with and let's progress to the next stage…

Stop and Filter Words

At this stage it is important to make sure that your key phrase contains no "Stop" or "Filter" words. Stop words will cause the search engine spider to completely stop the indexing process; these are usually adult or censored words. Filter words are those which are so commonly used that they have become ineffective, such as "the", "for", "a" and so on. These words are removed from websites by search engines before they are added to their databases, and so are always ignored. For example, let's say that you own a Guest House in Newquay, Cornwall, called Surfside Lodge. You might be inclined to use the keyword phrase:

Surfside Lodge is a Guest House in Newquay where you can Surf

In this instance, you would need to remove the Filter words "is", "a", "in", "where", "you", and "can".

Keyword Phrases

Using the example above, we are left with the words:

Surfside Lodge Guest House Newquay Surf

The next step is to rearrange these keywords into workable phrases. "Surfside Lodge" is a good phrase but would only be effective if people were specifically searching for your accommodation. "Guest House" is useful as it is likely to be frequently searched for. "Newquay Surf" might be better phrased "Surf Newquay" as people will probably search for "Surf" before "Newquay".

The keywords you choose will determine the kind of traffic you get.

If your keyword is "Surf Newquay" you are likely to attract people interested in surf or surfing in Newquay, and if you were to use the keyword "Guest House Family" you may not appeal to young surfers.

In generating keywords you will need to consider the kind of traffic you want to attract. We advise that you use three techniques. Firstly, you should brainstorm, as illustrated opposite, with friends and colleagues as many potential keywords as possible. It may help to try and think like a potential customer. You should then ask your existing customers what keywords they would use in search engines. Only then should you look at your competitors' sites. By applying these three techniques you will have generated enough keywords to start an analysis using tools as described earlier in this chapter.

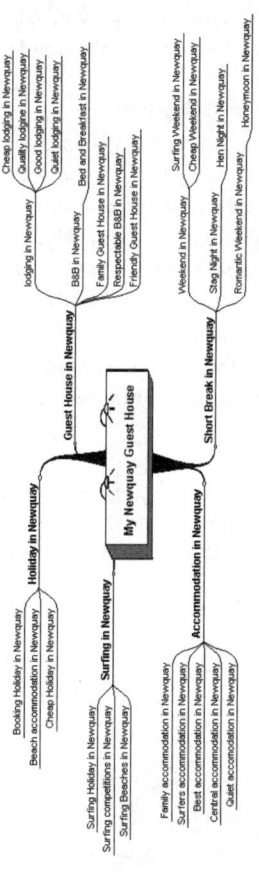

Keywords < 11

(Note: It may help at this point for you to look at Chapter 5, in the section entitled "Keywords Working Harder".)

Competitor Analysis

Now, using the keywords that you have anticipated that your customers may be using, go to some search engines and try using some of these and see what results you get.

Are the results relevant to your business? If yes, then you've found your keyword competition and it's definitely worth going through these websites with a fine-tooth comb. Make a note of any SEO principles they may have used. This should not only keep you abreast of what techniques others are using to succeed, but hopefully will give you a few new ideas for keywords.

You may find it helpful to use a table to list keywords, competitors and techniques. An example of such a table is shown on the next page.

Website	Position Builder
URL	http://www.position-builder.com
Found in search engines	AltaVista, Excite, Lycos, Yahoo, Fast, GoTo, NBCi, LookSmart, MSN, Google
Keywords	Web Site Promotion Search Engine Ranking
Methods used	Gateways and Doorways, ALT tags, absolute links, H1 tags, site map
Ideas gathered from website	Use absolute links, use keywords in H1 tags, use a site map and submit it to search engines

Define Weighting

Now that you have your keywords arranged into phrases, it is time to rank them in order of importance. The spider ranks the words from left to right, the left hand being the most important. The first phrase is known as the "Primary Keyword Phrase", the next the "Secondary Keyword Phrase" and so on. Continuing with our example, a good phrase order would be:

Guest House Surf Newquay Surfside Lodge

"Guest House" should come first, as the people you are trying to attract firstly need to be looking for accommodation, which is what your site is all about. Secondly they need to be looking for somewhere to surf, as this is the central reason why people stay at your Guest House. As Newquay is a well-known surfing resort this will also be a popular keyword. The name of your business should come last as it is unlikely that people will type in "Surfside Lodge" as a search enquiry.

Keyword Density

It is important that individual words are not repeated too frequently in your keyword phrases, not more than three or four times at the most, and less if possible. If you find that you do have a high proportion of a particular word, try changing it into a variation of its stem word, for example "Surf" could be altered to "Surfs", "Surfer" or "Surfing". The spider will read all of these as completely different words and this will help to avoid the problem of repetition. We will be returning to the subject of keyword density later in the guide.

Conclusion

Through reading this chapter you will hopefully have discovered how important keywords are, which ones to use for your own business and how to organise them effectively. In the next chapter we will begin to tell you some of the other important ways of getting your site to the top of search engine listings.

3
Design Optimisation

The Importance of Good Design

Achieving good listings in the search engines is a matter of balance. It is vital for your website to be well optimised, that is, to contain all your keywords in the right places. This will certainly help it to rank highly. But of equal importance is its design and appearance. You want your site to be both easy to find and visually appealing to potential customers. This chapter deals with many fundamental aspects of design optimisation and will help you to organise the structure and wording of your website to your best advantage.

Not *all* search engines will respond to *all* of the following methods.

Title

Let's make one thing clear: the title of your website *has* to be optimised. The title is the part of the HTML code between the title tags:

<title>Keyword</title>

This is the first place from which the spider gathers keywords and so it is vital that yours are included. If they are not, you might as well give up now! Going back to our example from the last chapter, a badly optimised title would be:

<title>Surfside Lodge</title>

A correctly optimised title might be:

<title>guest house newquay cornwall surfing</title>

This is because people are more likely to search for a Guest House in Newquay in Cornwall than to search using the words Surfside Lodge. In summary, make sure that all your keyword phrases are listed in your title, preferably in the order you think people are likely to type in. A final word of advice: try to make your title pleasing to the eye of an Internet user. For example:

<title>guest house newquay cornwall at the surfside lodge</title>

This will be effective for both the search engines and any potential visitors to your site.

Meta Tags

The Meta Tags are written within the head of an HTML document. The head is something which a spider would read, but which the browser cannot see, as it appears above the website in the HTML code. There are two kinds of Meta Tag. The first is the keywords Meta Tag, which is written in the code as follows:

<meta name = "keywords" content = "keywords">

Where a word is underlined in the HTML code, it means the word should be subsitituted by the things to which the word refers. For example, in the code above, keywords should be replaced by the actual keywords themselves.

The description Meta Tag looks like this:

<meta name = "description" content = "keywords">

Many people still believe that these are the be all and end all of search engineering. This is simply not true! In fact, if improperly used, Meta Tags can actually hinder your website's position rather than help it. Outlined below are some good general rules for their use. It is important to note at this point that only certain search engines, for example HotBot and AltaVista, index Meta Tag information.

- Do not over-repeat your keywords in the Meta Tags – any more than three times is too many. Try stemming your words (as outlined in Chapter 2 in the section entitled "Keyword Density") to avoid being penalised by the search engines.

- It is important to include a description Meta Tag. If you don't do this, the search engine will either create its own description, or pull a description from the first few lines of text on your website. If these first few lines do not accurately reflect the main theme of your site, this will obviously damage your chances of a high listing. Therefore your description Meta Tag needs to be relevant to both your company and your keywords, and should not be more than 250 words long. However, some search engines completely disregard the description Meta Tag and do pull the first few lines of body content from your website. It is therefore important to make sure the first few lines of text on your website are suitable to be displayed as your description. For example:

```
...
<meta name = "description" content =
"Looking for a Guest House in Newquay?
Want to go Surfing? Come to the Surfside
Lodge!">

</html>
<body>

<b> Looking for a Guest House in Newquay?
Want to go Surfing? Come to the Surfside
Lodge!</b>

<table>...
```

- There is no strict limit to the number of words you can use in your keywords Meta Tag. However, it is worth remembering that some search engines will only read the first 250 characters of the HTML, including all commas, spaces and so on. Another point to keep in mind is that the more words you use the less impact your primary keywords will have, as their effect will be diluted.

- Some website engineers may recommend using commas to break up your keywords into separate phrases. Our opinion is that this should be avoided if possible. (See

Chapter 5 in the section entitled "Keywords Working Harder".)

- Avoid using irrelevant keywords in your Meta Tags. It may be tempting to throw in an unrelated but popular phrase in an attempt to attract more potential customers to your site. (For example using "Britney Spears" as a keyword for a site about plant pots.) This will not be looked upon favourably and may lead to your site being rejected by the search engines. Aside from this, it will probably not be an effective way of attracting customers.

- Do not use any keywords in the Meta Tag that do not appear in your main website, as they will not be effective in all search engines.

- There has been a lot of confusion about the law and keywords, and the use of trademarks and copyrighted names in Meta Tags. The truth is, there is no set law, as is the case with most of the Internet. There have been companies in the past who have been taken to court because they have been accused of using registered trademarks for their keywords. Some are accused of trying to steal traffic, for instance you could have a site selling computers, and then put in a word like Microsoft in your keywords, which is related to the website. Other websites may very well just fill up their keywords with company name after company name, just to get any sort of traffic. Some cases which are taken to court win, some lose.

Play safe, and don't use registered trademarks or copyrighted names.

Body Content

The body content is the main text of your website. It appears in the HTML code between the tags:

<body>_</body>

It is important that your body content relates to the words you have chosen for your keywords and Meta Tags. Your grasp of the English language is important here; your text needs to be both professionally written and keyword dense. As a rule, seven to eight per cent of your text needs to be made up of your keywords.

Avoid "Spamming" or "Keyword Stuffing", that is, repeating your keywords over and over in the text in an effort to gain a higher listing. If you do this your site will be completely rejected by the search engines. It also looks very unprofessional and will not impress a potential customer.

Some businesses may have the problem that they specialise in two very different services. Say, for example, that your site sells televisions and radiators. There is an obvious theme conflict here; having both of these words as your keywords will confuse the spider. The solution here is to create two separate web pages, each dealing with one individual subject, rather than putting them together. For some search engines, the body content is the most important aspect of the website, so taking the time to get it right is crucial.

Images

Images are clearly an important aspect of a website as they make it more appealing to the viewer. Unfortunately, even if your image is full of your keywords, a spider will take no notice of it. There are two possible solutions to this problem.

- When you save the image, the computer will ask you to give it a name. Giving it a name that is one of your keywords will ensure that the spider reads it.

- Some computers are unable to display website images. In their place will be an "ALT tag".

For example, in the space where a picture of a plant pot would be there might be a piece of text reading, "This is a picture of a plant pot". This text space is useful – you can fill it with your keywords and the spider will read them!

 keyword 1 keyword 2 keyword 3

Links

Links on a website will be in the form of either images or text. We recommend that you use textual links rather than image links because the spider can follow them much more easily and they also count as keywords. (More information about links can be found in Chapter 4 in the section entitled "Link Popularity".)

Tables

Humans read text on a page in a different way to spiders. The following illustration demonstrates the two different perspectives:

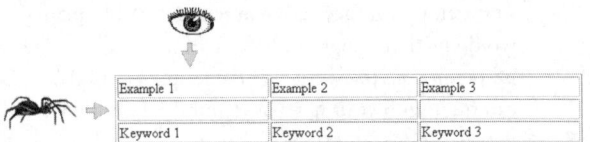

The human eye reads down the table, but the spider reads across. Therefore it takes the spider longer to find the first keyword in the text. The empty spaces in the table are known as "Blank Cells". It is best to keep these to a minimum, particularly at the top of your web page because you want the spider to find lots of your keywords in the first few lines of text. The spider will only index these first few lines and if there are not many of your keywords here your site will not be listed highly in the search enquiry results.

Text Formatting

Spiders rate some types of text as more important than others. The Header (the main title of your site) is the most important in terms of search engineering and should include one of your keywords. There are three Header tags, known in the code as H1 (<h1>keyword</h1>), H2 (<h2>keyword</h2>) and H3 (<h3>keyword</h3>). H1 is the main heading of your site and is therefore the most important. The Headers are followed in importance respectively by bold text (keyword), underlined text (<u>keyword</u>) and italic text (<I>keyword</I>).

It is a good idea to play with the keywords on your website using these different formats, as this will improve the position of your search engine listing.

Frames

While browsing on the web, you have probably seen separate Internet pages which have been placed together on the screen to appear as one. These separate pages are known as "Frames".

To put several of these together, you need a small piece of the HTML code known as the "Frameset", which looks like this:

```
<FRAMESET>
<NO FRAMES>KEYWORD</NO FRAMES>

<FRAME src = "main htm" name = "keyword">
</FRAMESET>
```

The Frameset places the separate pages together, as seen below.

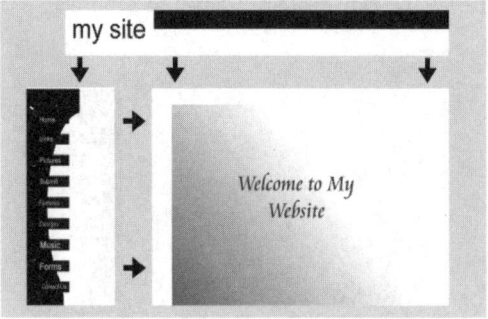

Now all the pages have been placed together to create a web page that can be used in most browsers.

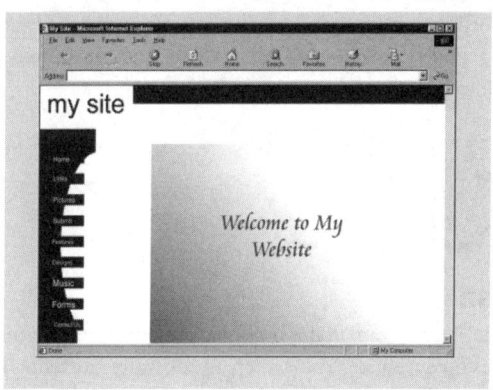

As you can see, this Frameset has a "No Frames" tag in it. If your Internet browser does not support Frames, this No Frames tag will read:

<NO FRAMES> YOUR BROWSER DOES NOT SUPPORT FRAMES, PLEASE FIND A BROWSER THAT WILL. </NO FRAMES>

When you submit a Frames page to a search engine, the spider will look through the No Frames tag. Therefore it is a good idea to fill this tag with your keywords. This way, instead of reading "Your browser does not support Frames" etc, the spider will read and index all of your keywords. Another tip is to give each Frame a keyword name. These keywords should be written into the Frameset as pictured above. In fact, the more keywords you can put in here the better because the Frameset is the actual piece of the HTML code that gets submitted to the search engine.

Most search engines will not index a framed site.

Flash

"Flash" is a program that is used to create interactive or moving images on a website. You can create an entire site using Flash, including all of your links and the main body of your text. This is becoming an increasingly popular feature, as it can look very impressive and attractive. The disadvantage of using it is that no matter how eye catching and keyword-dense your Flash images are, the search engine spider will not index them. If you do decide to create your website entirely in Flash, it is a good idea to have a separate HTML version of your site so that you will not lose your search engine position.

Conclusion

This chapter has examined some of the most important methods of optimising your website. Putting these into practice is the first step towards improving your position in search engine listings. In the following chapter we will look at some further ways of doing this by using "Doorways" and "Gateways".

4

Doorways and Gateways

What are Doorways?

A Doorway is a web page targeted for one keyword phrase usually registered under a different domain name. Essentially, however, it is an extension of your site. Visitors to your Doorway page will either find that it contains a link into your main site, or they will be automatically redirected into it. Doorways are designed to be keyword-dense in order that they will rank highly within the search engines under a specific phrase. The general idea is that if the Doorway page has a high ranking, it is likely to be noticed by your potential customers, who will then use it to click through into your main website.

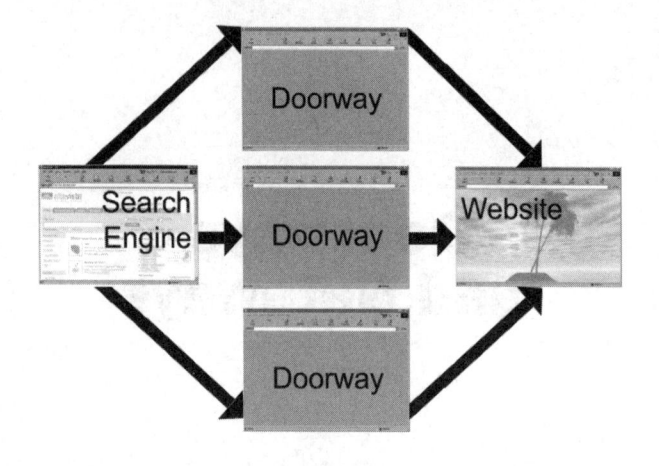

What are Gateways?

A Gateway is another separate web page containing a huge list of links to all the pages of your main site, including your Doorway pages. Gateways do not need to rank highly within the search engines and are not designed to be attractive to Internet users. Their sole purpose is to appeal to the spider. The way this works is fairly simple. Instead of submitting each of your pages to the search engine, you submit only your Gateway page. When a spider comes across your Gateway page, it *should* follow all the links to your main site. The benefit of this is that some search engines give higher rankings to pages that the spider finds on its own rather than those submitted directly by you.

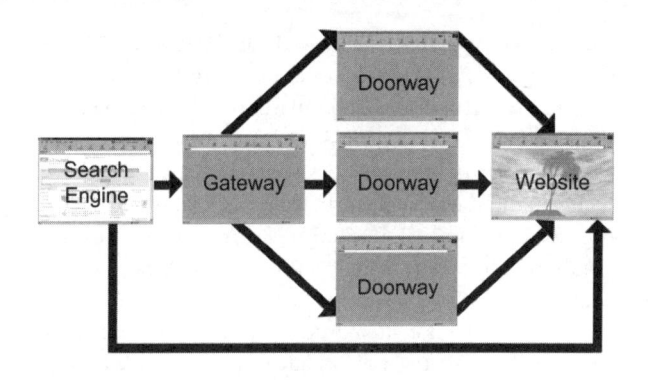

The Importance of Doorways and Gateways

Doorways are particularly useful for companies who promote a large number of products or services online. It is clearly not possible for such companies to optimise their main web page for keywords relating to each individual product. Their Doorway pages can focus on specific product keywords and can then lead into the main site. Doorways are also useful if you have your main site fully optimised using three of your key phrases, but you have a good fourth phrase you would like to use.

Designing a Doorway Page

The key to designing a Doorway page is to treat it as a mini website. It is possible for every page of your site to be a Doorway page. Therefore the same rules which you apply when creating your main site should be applied to your Doorway page: keywords and phrases need to be carefully chosen, body content has to be optimised and all the normal search engineering principles should be followed. Doorway pages do not really need to look too spectacular, as their sole purpose is to rank highly in the search engines. However is it worth making the page look professional; it is unlikely that people will use it to click through to your main site if it looks bad. Keep the text content of your Doorway page relevant to the theme(s) of your main site and do not attempt to spam the page. Each search engine will decide for itself whether or not you are trying to spam them, but as long as you are sensible with your keywords you shouldn't have any problems.

> **BEWARE**
> Don't submit your Doorway pages to a directory. Directories will only list one page of your site in their index, and you want them to index your main site.

Designing a Gateway Page

First, pull together all the links you have, to your main website or to your Doorway pages and put them in an HTML file. You will need to use the robots Meta Tag here. This is a very specific piece of code in the head of your document that tells the spider (or "robot") which pages you want indexed and which links should be followed. The Gateway page code should read:

> Do not index me but follow the lin[k]
>
> <meta name= "robots" content= "noinde[x"]

This means that you are telling the spider no[t to index the] site, but to follow all the links on the page. Keep y[our] page concise, simple and useful. Make sure that all [link]s on the page, as well as the domain name, are made up of key phrases that are relevant to your main site. Remember, however, there is no guarantee that a spider visiting your Gateway will follow the links on the page.

Link Popularity

The competition between the search engines is becoming increasingly fierce as they are all trying to provide their customers with the best quality websites. One way in which they do this is by noting the number of links there are to your site. The hypothesis is that the more links there are, the more popular (and therefore higher quality) your site must be. As a result your site should achieve a higher ranking. There are a number of ways to improve your link popularity, some of which are more reliable than others. There are an increasing number of online companies offering you a lot of links; these are known as "Link Farms" (See Chapter 9). However, these are generally a bad idea; the lists that they submit your site to are often completely irrelevant to your own site and can actually damage your search engine position. There are several other methods of improving your link popularity:

Build a Gateway page containing links both to your own site and to any pages of other companies' sites that contain links to you.

- Email other Internet companies which are similar to your own. (You can find these by using a directory such as Yahoo.) Send them a personalised message explaining what link popularity is and how it could benefit them, and asking them if they would like to trade links. You could offer to let them use some of the material from your website on their own site if they agree to give you a link in return.

- Check your link popularity at www.marketposition.com and sign up for their free newsletter. They will inform you of any changes in your link popularity.

- Post your URL on message boards, newsgroups etc – as many places as possible, and ask other people if they would like to trade links.

The best general advice is to begin by developing a good quality website. If others see you as a quality company, you might well find that many of them are linking to you already. Remember, the purpose of having more links is not only so that people will click on them, but also to appeal to the spider, so that your search engine position will improve.

5
Tips and Tricks

Before we begin, a note of warning: the tips and tricks described below, whilst often highly beneficial to your search engine rankings, could also adversely affect the position of your website. Remember that all search engines work quite differently; what is effective in one could mean disaster in another! Also, in some search engines these techniques will have no effect at all. However, they are worth knowing about because many sites have gained high positions using them.

Planning for each Search Engine

For effective search engineering you need to plan and know how each search engine will treat your site. Perhaps the best way is having SEO strategies that are specific to each search engine. So, provided you have read all the information in this guide about the search engines, you should be able to create different Doorways for AltaVista and Excite. This should help your rankings because each Doorway is specifically designed to complement the way each individual search engine spider crawls.

The Invisible Pixel

Invisible pixels are tiny (1 pixel by 1 pixel), transparent "images" which can be positioned anywhere on your site. They are too small to be seen by the human eye, but are very useful, as the piece of code which is assigned to them can be used to add extra keywords on to your page. They can also be made into a link to another Gateway page. By adding your keywords into the <IMG ALT=> tag, you will have loaded the invisible pixel "image". Although it will take up only the tiniest possible space on your web page, the spider will read the keywords and should index your site more highly as a result.

> It may be tempting to use hundreds of these invisible pixels to add extra keywords to your page, but it isn't a good idea, as the search engines will soon notice that you are trying to spam them! Stick to one or two at the most.

Absolute Links

These are links on your web pages that are registered under separate domain names. In actual fact, however, they only lead to other pages of your own site. These links are designed to fool the spider into thinking it is leaving your site and going to another one. This increases your link popularity, because the spider assumes that these other "sites" must be popular when it sees that you have links to them on your own web page. Consequently it ranks them more highly.

Hidden Text

You may discover, having designed your website, that it is lacking in text content and so is not as keyword-rich as it needs to be. Putting in hidden text is one way to increase your keyword density. This is achieved by putting your keywords within your main web page but making them the same colour as the background so that they are invisible. For example, if you want your hidden text to be white, set the background colour thus:

    <BGCOLOUR= "#FFFFFF">

and the font colour thus:

    <fontcolour= "#FFFFFF">

There is one problem with this: spiders are becoming very clever. They can detect that your text and background are the same colour, and some of them don't appreciate you trying to trick them! A possible way around this is to use semi-invisible text. To do this you need to change the colour of the text very slightly, so that it is still hidden from the naked eye, but *should* appear to the spider as a different colour. Using the above example, you would keep the background white, but change the font colour to off white:

<fontcolour= "#FEFEFE">

Unfortunately this is still not always effective; spiders are beginning to detect the different levels of colour, and some will penalise you as a result of this. For full information on how to set your text and background colours, see the "help" contents of your HTML editing program where you should find everything you need to know.

> **BEWARE**
> Keep in mind that if you decide to use this technique, you need to avoid spamming your invisible text – your website visitors may not see the same words repeated over and over, but the spider will!

Hidden Links

The purpose of hidden links is to get more of your web pages ranked by the search engines. Spiders should follow, and index, all the links they find on a web page, and for this reason it is good to include *all* of your links on *every* page of your site. However, it doesn't really look too professional to have masses

of links on your web pages, so it is a good idea to c
links. These are basically the same as absolute link
but are created using the same method as hidde
explained above). If your site has a large number of pages, then one method of getting each one indexed is to put the same hidden link on every page. This one link should lead to a contents page listing all of your other pages. This way, you can ensure that the spider will index everything you want it to.

ASCII

Some search engines use ASCII, a word rating system that ranks certain characters more highly than others. The ranking order, from highest to lowest, is as follows:

!"#$%&'()*+,-./0123456789:;<=>?@ABCDEFGHIJKL MNOPQRSTUVWXYZ`abcd

and so on. If you add these characters to the beginning of your keywords then your site will be rated more highly, even if your keywords are lower in the ranking than those of your rivals. For example "! Plant Pots UK" would receive a higher position than "American Plant Pots". Try to keep your ASCII keywords reasonably attractive to web users; don't use hundreds of them in an attempt to get a higher listing. As with any other trick, search engines are beginning to pick up on it, so be sensible!

Keywords Working Harder

It is a good idea to arrange your keywords in a way that allows you to get the maximum possible number of phrase combinations from them. For example, if you run a website that sells books online, then your obvious key phrases will be "books online" and "online books". However, combining the two to create the phrase "books online books" will give you two of your most important key phrases using only three words. If you use this technique then you need to avoid putting commas between your keywords, as this will prevent the spider from reading them as one continuous phrase.

Comment Tags

Comment tags are small messages and notes in the HTML code from one web designer to another. They look like this:

<!— Your comment here—>

They are useful because they are not seen by the general web user and can be filled with your keywords. Also, if you place them right at the top of your code, the spider will index them before anything else.

> Not all spiders will read this information and some search engines (AltaVista, Excite, Infoseek, WebCrawler, Lycos and HotBot) will completely dismiss it. This could even lead to them dismissing your site as a whole.

Your best bet is to use this principle on Doorway pages, because at the end of the day, the URL of your Doorway page can be changed whereas your main URL cannot, so test a few Doorways before using this idea globally.

Cascading Style Sheets (CSS)

Cascading style sheets enable you to put ordinary sized text, which can appear anywhere on your website, into the Header tag. The Header is the first place from which the spider gathers keywords, as it appears right at the top of the HTML code. It is normally used to indicate the size, colour etc of your site's heading. However, in this instance, you use it to store keywords from the main body of your site's text, so that the spider thinks they are very important and indexes them before anything else. To do this, you need to add a line to your H1 tag similar to the one below, although font style and size can be changed to whatever you like:

h1   { font-family: Verdana, Arial, Helvetica, sans-serif; font-size: 10px; font-style: normal}

Then place your *real* heading in the following code:

<H1>Your headline text here</H1>

This may be helpful in some search engines as a way to boost your site's position.

Another good reason for using cascading style sheets is that you don't clog the spider with unnecessary code. Without cascading style sheets you would have a lot of code defining the colour of the links, background, etc within your website. By using cascading style sheets you reduce the amount of code, which means a spider will get to the keywords in your body content quicker, which will increase the likelihood of getting a better position.

In the next chapter we will explain some further tips and tricks that can be used to improve search engine rankings, as well as some of the pitfalls to avoid when optimising your website.

6

Advanced Techniques

This chapter looks at some of the further techniques that have been used to improve search engine rankings.

> **BEWARE**
> We would not suggest that you necessarily use these methods, and in fact some of them should definitely be avoided. This chapter is as much about telling you what *not* to do as what to do.

However, it is likely that some of your competitors are using these tricks to get to the top, so it's a good idea for you to at least be aware of them.

JavaScript Redirection

When a web user clicks into a particular site or page, they may occasionally find that they are immediately transferred to another site with a different domain address. This is also known as "Auto Redirection" or "Meta Refresh". The latter has been used and abused a great deal which means that nowadays most search engines seriously frown upon it. One slightly better method is to use JavaScript code, which automatically redirects the browser to a different page, after the page has loaded. The code looks like this:

```
<SCRIPT language="javaScript1.1">
<!—
location.replace(http.//www.domain.com);
//
</SCRIPT>
```

Using this method has its disadvantages. Some spiders may follow the redirection links, but will not necessarily index the original page. Also, the spider reads the JavaScript code first, so your website text (along with all your keywords!) is moved lower in the source code. This means that your page may not rank as highly for keyword density as it otherwise would.

> This technique should not be used when submitting to directories, as a human editor will *not* index pages that use redirection.

> Many search engines will ignore JavaScript commands.

Cloaking

This is when two or more different web pages are served from the same address. One page is designed for human visitors, and the other is optimised for the particular search engine spider that you want to appeal to.

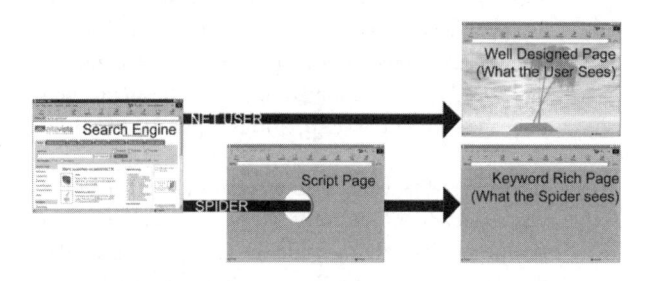

This has two advantages; firstly, in the "human" page, the source code can be hidden. This is a great benefit to you if your site promotes a very popular product or service, because your competitors cannot look at your code to see how you optimised your site. Secondly, the "spider" page does not have to look attractive to web users and so it can be fully optimised using all of your keywords.

> Using this technique requires quite a lot of skill, as you need to be familiar with CGI Script writing.

There are two methods of cloaking:

- Agent Name Delivery: Every search engine has a name for its spider (AltaVista's is "Scooter", Inktomi's is "Slurp", and so on). These names are listed in the CGI Script (a computer program containing the names and IP numbers of all the search engine spiders). So for example, when AltaVista's spider comes to index your site, the CGI server will see that the name "Scooter" is on its list, and will automatically serve the engine with the page that you have specifically optimised for it.

- IP Address Delivery: This works in almost the same way as agent name delivery. Every search engine has an IP number identifying it and the CGI Script lists all of these numbers. It can identify which spider is visiting your site, and then serve the spider with the page you have created for that particular engine.

Robot Handling

Sometimes it may become important to prevent access to certain parts of your server or website.

You may have a section of your website that is being developed or you may simply have a part of your site that you do not want indexed (eg a jokes page). You may also have within your website pages optimised for a specific search engine and as such don't want other search engine spiders to index or even view them. This can be accomplished using the methods detailed below.

It is possible for you to have total control over the spiders (or robots) that visit your website, including where they go and what they do, by using the robots.txt file. This is the first thing that the spider looks for when it visits your site. It can be created using any text editor and then added to the very top of your site with the permission of your website host. Below are some examples of the instructions you will need to use.

> Remember to use lower case letters throughout the robots.txt file.

1. To exclude all spiders from the server:

   User-agent: *
   Disallow: /

2. To allow all spiders free access:

   User-agent: *
   Disallow:

3. To exclude all spiders from parts of a server:

   User-agent: *
   Disallow: /cgi-bin/
   Disallow: /tmp/
   Disallow: /private/

4. To prevent access of a single spider:

   User-agent: <u>(enter name of spider)</u>
   Disallow: /

> **HOT TIP:** This is obviously a very useful file to create, as it puts you in control of what parts of your site are indexed. It will also enable you to know when a spider has visited your site.

Presto Chango

This is a fairly simple technique, and it can be effective in some cases. The first thing to do is to design a page for submission to the specific search engine of your choice. It does not have to look attractive, as long as it contains all of your keywords in the right places so that the engine will rank it as highly as possible.

The idea is that once this page has been indexed highly, you can swap it for your *real* web page – the one that you want all your potential customers and visitors to see. This is not necessarily a recommended way to improve your rankings, but it is still quite popular, and might well be one of the tricks that your competitors have used to get to the top.

Spamming

As we mentioned earlier in the guide, spamming is a bad idea – avoid it at all costs! You might be tempted to try it, particularly if you notice that some of your competitors seem to have used it successfully to get a high ranking. However, even if they are getting away with it at the moment, they are sure to be punished for it sooner or later, and you don't want to follow in their footsteps! Spamming is likely to result in your site losing its ranking, if not being banned altogether. The search engines vary in what they consider to be spam, but there are some general rules you should follow.

1. Do not repeat your keywords over and over again, either in your main site, your Meta Tags, title, or anywhere else. This is not only spam, but it is also likely to put off any potential customers who visit your site.

2. Do not use irrelevant but popular keywords in an effort to get a higher listing – the spider will soon pick up on this!

3. Do not create too many Doorway pages – if your main site has only eight pages, you do not need 28 Doorway pages leading to it. Use your common sense to decide how many you really need.

Hidden Form Fields

While browsing the web, you have probably come across forms that you can fill in online. The <input> Hidden tag is used in the code for these types of forms, and this tag can be used to add extra hidden keywords to your page. The HTML code looks like this:

<INPUT TYPE= "HIDDEN" NAME= "hidden" VALUE= "type your keywords here">

> Don't use a long string of keywords in this part of the code – form them into a clear sentence, to avoid being penalised for spamming.

7
The Search Engines

It is estimated that most Internet visitors use one of the top 15 search engines to search for the kind of websites they want. With this in mind, it is a good idea to learn a bit about the background of the major search engines and the different ways in which they operate.

altavista
THE SEARCH COMPANY

www.altavista.com

AltaVista is consistently one of the largest search engines on the web, in terms of pages indexed. Its comprehensive coverage and wide range of power searching commands makes it a particular favourite among researchers. In addition to crawler-based web page matches, it also offers news search, shopping search, multimedia search and human-powered directory results from LookSmart (see below). AltaVista opened in December 1995. It was owned by Digital, then run by Compaq (which purchased Digital in 1998). It then spun off into a separate company that is now controlled by CMGI.

AOL

www.aol.com

AOL Search allows its members to search across both the web and AOL's own content from one place. The "external" version, listed above, does not list AOL content. The main listings for categories and websites come from the Open Directory (see below). Inktomi (see below) also provides crawler-based results, as backup to the directory information. Before the launch of AOL Search in October 1999, the AOL search service was Excite-powered AOL NetFind.

www.ask.co.uk

Ask Jeeves is a human-powered search service that aims to direct you to the exact page that answers your question. If it fails to find a match within its own database, then it will provide matching web pages from various search engines.

www.directhit.com

Direct Hit measures what people click on in the search results presented at its own site and at its partner sites, such as HotBot (see below). Sites that get clicked on more than others rise higher in Direct Hit's rankings. Thus, the service dubs itself a "popularity engine". Aside from running its own website, Direct Hit provides the main results that appear at HotBot and is available as an option to searchers at MSN Search. Direct Hit is owned by Ask Jeeves.

excite

www.excite.com

Excite offers a medium-sized crawler-based web page index, as well as access to human-powered directory results from LookSmart. Excite was launched in late 1995. It grew quickly in prominence and consumed two of its competitors, Magellan in July 1996, and WebCrawler in November 1996. These continue to run as separate services.

fast

www.alltheweb.com

Formerly called All The Web, FAST Search aims to index the entire web. It was the first search engine to break the 200 million web page index milestone and consistently has one of the largest indexes of the web. The Norwegian company behind FAST Search also powers some of the results that appear at Lycos (see below). FAST Search launched in May 1999.

Google

www.google.com

Google is a search engine that uses link popularity as its primary method of ranking websites. This can be especially helpful in finding good quality sites in response to general searches such as "cars" and "travel", because users across the web have essentially voted for the best sites by linking to them. The system works so well that Google has gained widespread praise for its relevancy. Google also has a huge index of the web and provides some results to Yahoo and Netscape Search.

www.goto.com

Unlike the other major search engines, GoTo sells its main listings. Companies can pay money to be placed higher in the search results, which GoTo feels improves the relevancy.

Non-paid results come from Inktomi. GoTo launched in 1997 and incorporated the former University of Colorado-based World Wide Web Worm. In February 1998, it shifted to its current pay-for-placement model and soon after replaced the WWW Worm with Inktomi for its non-paid listings. Paid listings from GoTo also appear on other major search engines, including AltaVista, AOL Search, Lycos, HotBot and Netscape Search.

HOTBOT

www.hotbot.com

HotBot is a favourite among researchers due to its many power-searching features. In most cases, HotBot's first page of results comes from the Direct Hit service and secondary results come from the Inktomi search engine, which is also used by other services. It gets its directory information from the Open Directory project. HotBot launched in May 1996 as Wired Digital's entry into the search engine market. Lycos purchased Wired Digital in October 1998 and continues to run HotBot as a separate search service.

Inktomi

Inktomi was originally a search engine at UC Berkeley. The creators then formed their own company using the same name and created a new Inktomi index, which was first used to power HotBot. The Inktomi index now also powers several other services, all of which tap into the same index. However, results may be slightly different, as Inktomi provides ways for its partners to use a common index yet distinguish themselves from other search engines. There is no way to query the Inktomi index directly, as it is only made available through Inktomi's partners with whatever filters and ranking tweaks they may apply.

looksmart

www.looksmart.com

LookSmart is a human-compiled directory of websites. In addition to its own independent service, it provides directory results for MSN Search, Excite and many others. LookSmart is provided with search results from Inktomi when a search fails to find a match from among their own reviews. Launched independently in October 1996, LookSmart was backed by Reader's Digest for approximately one year before company executives bought back control of the service.

LYCOS

www.lycos.com

Lycos started out as a search engine and relied on listings that came from spidering the web. In April 1999, it shifted to a directory model similar to Yahoo. Its main listings come from the Open Directory project, with secondary results from the FAST Search engine. Some Direct Hit results are also used. In October 1998, Lycos took over its competitor HotBot, which continues to be run separately.

msn

www.msn.com

Microsoft's MSN Search service is a LookSmart-powered directory of websites, with secondary results that come from Inktomi. RealNames and Direct Hit data is also made available.

NBCi

www.nbc.com

NBCi is a human-compiled directory of websites, supplemented by search results from Inktomi. It was formerly known as Snap but changed its name in late 2000. The directory is backed by US television network NBC. However, the future of the site is in doubt as NBC announced widespread layoffs in April 2001.

Northern Light

www.northernlight.com

Northern Light is another favourite search engine among researchers. It features a large index of the web, along with the ability to cluster documents by topic. Northern Light also has a set of "special collection" documents that are not readily accessible to search engine spiders. There are documents from thousands of sources, including newswires, magazines and

The Search Engines < 59

databases. Searching these documents is free, but there is a charge of up to $4 to view them. There is no charge to view documents on the public web – only for those within the special collection. Northern Light opened to general use in August 1997.

dmoz open directory project

www.dmoz.org

The Open Directory uses volunteer editors to catalogue the web. Formerly known as NewHoo, it was launched in June 1998. It was acquired by Netscape in November 1998, and the company pledged that anyone would be able to use information from the directory through an open licence arrangement. Netscape itself was the first licensee. Lycos and AOL Search also make heavy use of Open Directory data.

YAHOO!

www.yahoo.com

Yahoo is the web's most popular search service and has a well-deserved reputation for helping people find information easily.

The secret to Yahoo's success is human input; it is the largest human-compiled directory on the web, employing about 150 editors in an effort to place sites into individual categories. Yahoo has well over two million sites listed. It supplements its results with those from Google. If a search fails to find a match within Yahoo's own listings, then matches from Google are displayed. Google matches also appear after all Yahoo matches have first been shown. Yahoo is the oldest of the major website directories, having launched in late 1994.

Who Indexes What?

The sections below give a summary of some of the main features of the major search engines.

Crawling

The following table covers factors related to how well search engine spiders "crawl" websites.

Frames Support

This shows which search engines can follow frame links. Those that can't will probably fail to index much of your site. (See Chapter 3 for further information on how to deal with frames.)

Feature	Yes	No
Frames Support	All but...	FAST
Robots Meta Tag	All but...	Excite
Link Popularity	All	n/a
Revisits	AltaVista, Inktomi	Excite, FAST, Google, Northern Light
Paid Inclusion	Inktomi, LookSmart	Others

Robots Meta Tag
This is a special Meta Tag that allows site owners to specify any page(s) that shouldn't be indexed. (See Chapter 3 for more on Meta Tags.)

Link Popularity
All search engines can determine the popularity of a page by analysing how many links there are to it from other pages. Please note, however, that engines use this only as a means to determine which pages they will *include* in the index, NOT to determine the *ranking* that the pages will receive. (See below under "Link Popularity Boosts Ranking".)

Revisits
A number of search engines can learn how often pages change. Pages that change often may be visited more frequently.

Paid Inclusion
This shows which search engines offer guaranteed inclusion in their index in return for payment. However, the exact position you will attain in the index is not specified. (This is NOT the same as paid placement, which guarantees a particular position in relation to a particular search term.)

Indexing
The following table explains what gets indexed when search engines spider a page.

Full Body Text
All of the major search engines index the full visible body text of a page. Some will not index Stop words. (See Chapter 2, in the section entitled "Stop and Filter Words".)

Stop Words
Some search engines either leave out these words when they index a page or may not search for these words during a query. These Stop words are usually excluded as a way to save storage space or to speed up searches.

Feature	Yes	No
Full Body Text	All	n/a
Stop Words	AltaVista, Excite, Inktomi, Google	FAST, Northern Light
Description Meta Tag	All but...	FAST, Google, Northern Light
Keywords Meta Tag	All but...	Excite, FAST, Google, Northern Light
ALT Text	AltaVista, Google	Excite, FAST, Inktomi, Northern Light
Comments	Inktomi	Others

Description Meta Tag and Keywords Meta Tag

These show which search engines support these tags. (See Chapter 3, in the section entitled "Meta Tags".) This does NOT mean, however, that all search engines that support these tags give pages a ranking boost. This is covered below under "Meta Tags Boost Ranking".

ALT Text and Comments

This shows which search engines index ALT text associated with images, or text in comment tags.

Ranking

For most search engines, the ranking your site achieves is based on the location and frequency of the keywords on your web page. The exact mechanism is slightly different for each engine.

In addition to location and frequency, some engines may give a page a relevancy boost based on other factors. These can usually help to improve your ranking a little, but they don't guarantee a boost to the top. Some of the major factors are listed in the table below.

Feature	Yes	No
Meta Tags Boost Ranking	Inktomi	AltaVista, Excite, FAST, Google, Northern Light
Link Popularity Boosts Ranking	All, especially Google	n/a
Direct Hit Boosts Ranking	HotBot	Others

Meta Tags Boost Ranking

Some of the search engines that support the description and keywords Meta Tags will also give pages an extra boost if search terms appear in these areas. However, not all search engines that support the tags will also give a ranking boost.

Link Popularity Boosts Ranking

As mentioned earlier, all search engines can determine the popularity of a page by analysing how many links there are to it from other pages. However, some engines will actually give a rankings boost to sites that have lots of links, either on their own pages or from other significant websites (either large, well known companies or sites that are similar to your own). This is because they assume that sites with a large number of links must be popular, and therefore high quality.

Direct Hit Boosts Ranking

"Direct Hit" is a system that measures which sites people click on from their search results, and uses this to refine their relevancy rankings. This section of the table shows which search engines use this as a factor.

Spam

All the major search engines penalise sites that attempt to spam them in order to improve their position. One commonly used technique is "stacking" or "stuffing" words on a page; this is where the same keyword is repeated many times in a row. All the engines have their own idea of what constitutes spamming.

However, if they spot it, they may downgrade the ranking of your website or even exclude it from listings altogether. The table below covers the design elements that could result in a spam penalty.

Feature	Yes	No
Meta Refresh	AltaVista	Excite, FAST, Google, Inktomi, Northern Light
Invisible Text	Others	Excite, FAST, Google

Meta Refresh
Some site owners create target pages that automatically take visitors to different pages within a website. The meta refresh tag is often used to do this. For example, companies selling a variety of different products online may have specific target pages containing all the keywords for one particular product. Once this page is clicked into, users will be automatically directed into the main site. Some search engines will refuse to index a page with a high meta refresh rate. Google doesn't worry much about meta refresh tags because its link popularity ranking system pretty much defeats any attempts to spam it.

Invisible Text

This is the technique of placing keyword-dense text on a page in the same colour as the background, making it invisible to the human eye. This is for the purpose of improving search engine rankings by making the web page more keyword rich. However, as the table shows, many search engines will either refuse to index this text or will not index any page containing invisible text.

By now, you should have a good idea of the kinds of techniques that can be used to improve search engine listings, and you might feel that your site is fully optimised and ready for submission. If so, make sure you read the next chapter first! In it you will find tips on the best way to submit your site, and details of indexing times for all the major search engines.

8

Submission Tips

Final Check

Before you submit your site to the search engines, it is important that you check it thoroughly and make sure that you have completed all your search engineering. This is especially important because some search engines will only index you once: if you are indexed in the wrong category you could be stuck there! If you have spent a long time working on the design and search engineering of your site, it is well worth taking the extra time to follow the steps below.

Manual Submission

There are a growing number of online programmes offering to submit your website to the search engines. However, these are often a waste of time as the search engines they submit to are usually small and obscure. We strongly recommend that you submit your site yourself. This will enable you to choose the engines you would like to submit to. It is also looked upon favourably by the major search engines, who will see that you are making an effort and therefore take you more seriously.

Submit every major page of your site separately, and try if you can to submit no more than five pages per day.

> Directories will only index one page of your whole site and will use that page to decide which category to place you into, so make sure you submit your main web page to them. It may be impossible later to submit a different page.

How to Submit your Website

This section explains exactly how to submit your website to some of the top search engines and directories.

AltaVista

Submissions to AltaVista are protected by what is popularly called "The Ransom Note". The Ransom Note is a code generated by computers, and to submit to AltaVista, you need to input the code. The code changes each time a user goes to the submit page. AltaVista have developed this to prevent people creating macros to continually submit URLs to their index.

To submit, go to www.altavista.com/cgi-bin/newurl?, fill out the Ransom Note code, and submit your site, and after a period of up to one month, your site should be listed in the AltaVista index (if you follow the AltaVista guidelines given at www.altavista.com/sites/search/inc/sub_policy).

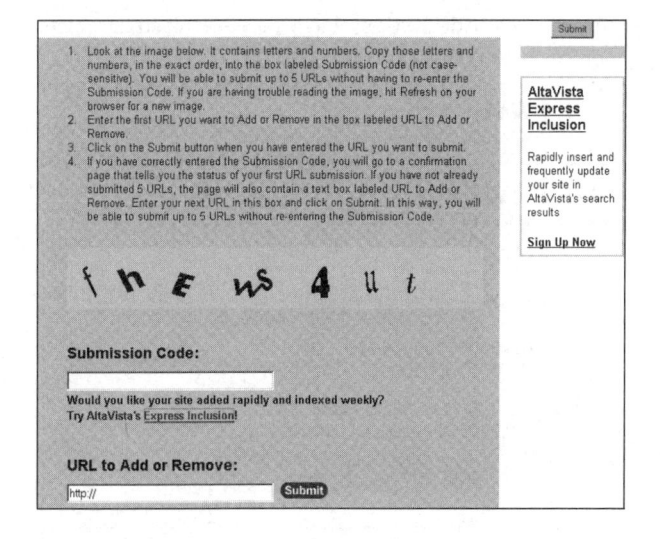

However, if you have the money, or need a listing quickly, you can express submit your site to AltaVista through InfoSpider (www.infospider.com). To sign up for this service, go to either www.infospider.com or alternatively you can go to www.altavista.com/sites/search/express_incl. The express submission sets your site as a priority to the AltaVista spider, and provided you adhere to the AltaVista policies (www.altavista.com/sites/search/inc/sub_policy), you should be in the AltaVista index within a week. However in the unlikely case you do have a problem, they do have an extremely good customer support team.

All The Web

alltheweb
all the web. all the time

Submit Your Site

Submitted sites will be scheduled for addition to AllTheWeb.com at the next update of the index. We do not add all submitted URLs to our index, and we cannot make any predictions or guarantees about when or if they will appear. For more information, please see the Webmasters FAQ.

Please enter your full URL, including the http:// prefix.
Please note: Only the top-level page from a host is necessary; you do not need to submit each individual page.

URL to add:	http://
Your email address:	
	Add URL

Front Page | Submit Your Site | Add AllTheWeb to Your Site | Contact FAST | Join the FAST Team | Help
powered by DELL servers   Copyright © 2001 Fast Search & Transfer ASA

To submit your site, go to www.alltheweb.com/add_url.php and fill out the forms, and as soon as they send out their spider the next time, you will be listed in their index!

Google

Google is perhaps the most respected search engine on the Internet, and to get listed, and listed high, is a great achievement. If you can do well in Google, you will have done well with your site SEO. So, go to www.google.com/addurl.html and fill out

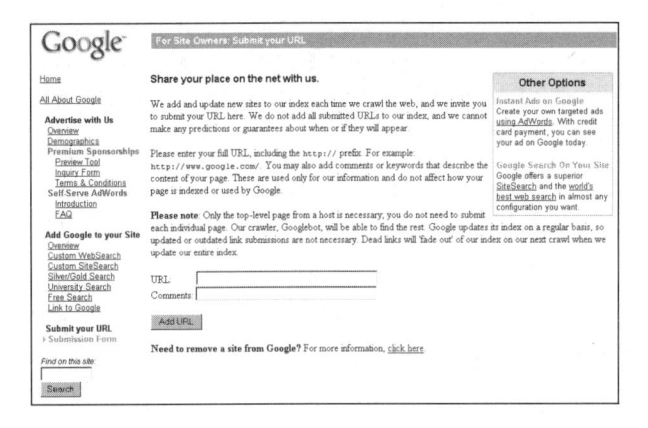

the form: all you need are comments and your URL. Hopefully, next time GoogleBot or BackRub (Google's spiders) are

Submission Tips < 73

dispatched across the web, you should get a listing, and hopefully a good one!

Yahoo

Submission to Yahoo is a bit more complicated because, after all, it is a directory, and URLs need to be placed in the correct place. So for instance, if your website is about computer retail, you would need to find the correct directory within Yahoo – go through these directories: Yahoo Main Page > Computers and Internet > Shopping and Services.

Once you have found the place where you want your site listed, on the bottom of the page is a link, "Suggest a Site". This takes you to a page where you have to fill out a comprehensive form which asks for:

- Site Title

- URL

- Description

- (Optional) Category Suggestion

- Contact Information

- Geographical Location

- Event Time of Site (if applicable)

- Final Comments

Once you have completed this form, pending human review, you should be in the Yahoo directory.

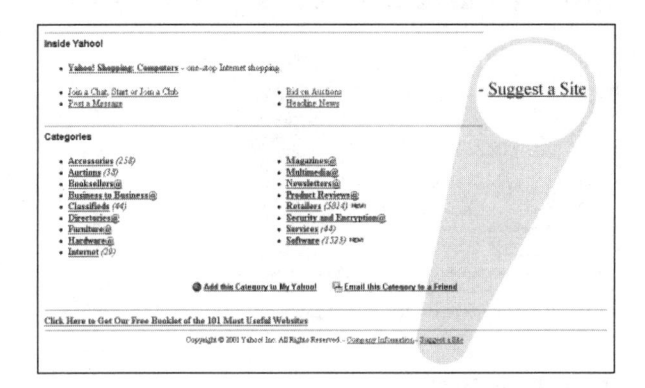

HotBot

Submitting to HotBot is extremely easy. You just go to hotbot.lycos.com/addurl.asp and fill out the form! It's as easy as that, and in up to three months your site will be listed in HotBot!

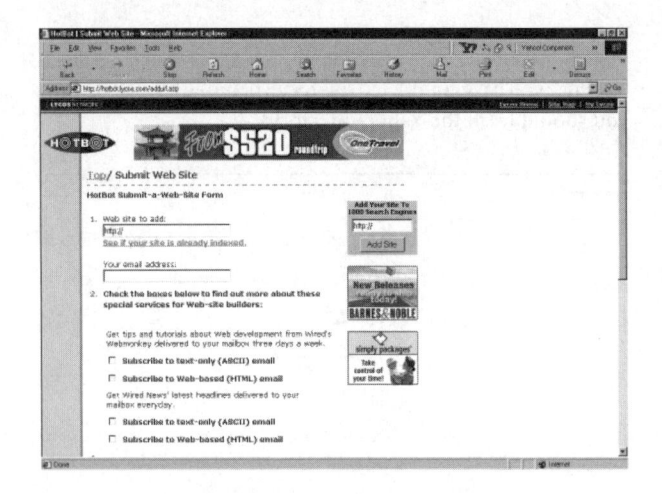

Open Directory

Submission to the Open Directory (www.dmoz.org) is similar to submission to Yahoo. Open Directory, like Yahoo, pride themselves on being highly selective, so users only get the best information available. Again, you have to find the appropriate category to submit to. Let's say your site is for a retail recruitment consultancy, so you would go through these directories: Business > Employment > Retail.

Then from there, you would click "add url", and fill out the form that appears, which asks for:

- URL

- Title of Site

- Site Description

- Email Address

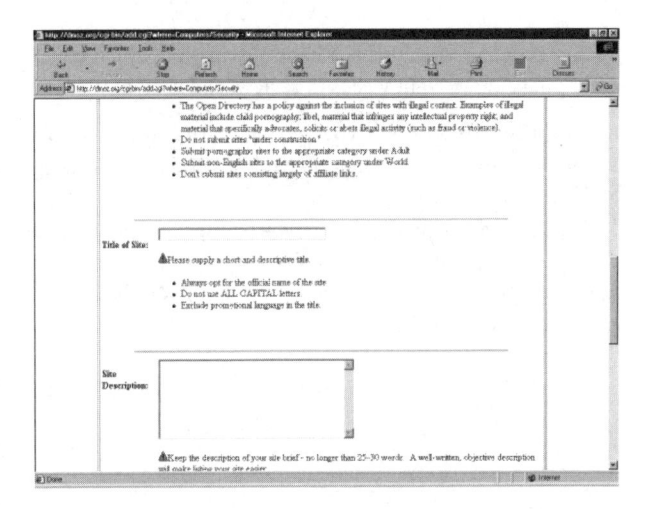

Then you need to accept their terms of use, given at dmoz.org/termsofuse.html and click "submit". Your site will then be given to an editor for approval.

LookSmart

LookSmart has three submission services:

1. Express Submit (one URL): for $199 this allows you to submit one URL that is reviewed within five days.

2. Submit Multiple URLs: allows you to submit multiple URLs, each URL costing $199!

3. Basic Submit: this is a basic submission which could take up to eight weeks to review, and costs $99.

In order to choose the service you want, go to submit.looksmart.com/info.jhtml?synd=US&chan=lshomepg and select your service.

However, the main problem is, you pay up your money, and there is no guarantee that your site will be listed, but if you adhere to their terms of use (click on the link on the submit page) you should be listed.

> **Drive Targeted Traffic to Your Web Site**
>
> Get new customers! Express Submit your site to leverage the massive reach of the LookSmart Network and the precision targeting of a search directory.
>
> - Reach 60 percent of UK Internet users through LookSmart's directory and its network of partners.
> - The LookSmart directory serves as the foundation for the directories of MSN (Microsoft Network), AltaVista, Excite@Home, NTL, Genie, World Online, BTopenworld and many more.
> - By submitting your site, you have the opportunity of unparalleled exposure across the web.
>
> ---
>
> **Get Listed Now With Express Submit** SM
>
> **Express Submit £149 GBP + VAT**
> - Guaranteed site review within **5 working days***
> - Listing in the most appropriate categories
>
> [Submit]
>
> * Within 5 working days you will be notified whether your site qualifies for inclusion in the directory. Please note that due to the varying update schedules of our partners, there may be some delay from receipt of this notification to when your site appears live in our directory on one of our partner sites. Please read our Submit a Site Guidelines.
>
> - Frequently Asked Questions
> - Customer Service

Excite

Excite, like LookSmart, has the option of an Express Submit. To make your selection go to www.excite.com/info/add_url and you will find buttons for the options available:

> **Drive Targeted Traffic to Your Web Site**
>
> Excite has partnered with LookSmart to offer Express Submit, the fast and easy way to submit your site to the Excite directory and the entire LookSmart Network.
>
> Your site will be listed in the LookSmart Network of partner sites including Excite, AltaVista, MSN, iWon, CNN, Time Warner, and over 370 ISPs. Excite and the LookSmart Network reach four out of five US Internet users - that's 64 million potential new customers!
>
> **Express Submit - Get Listed Fast!**
>
> - Guaranteed site review within two business days*
> - Your site submitted to the Excite directory and the rest of the LookSmart Network
> - Low one-time payment of $199 US
>
> [Express Submit]
>
> *Within two business days you will be notified whether your site qualifies for inclusion in the LookSmart Network, which includes the Excite directory.
>
> **Basic Submit**
>
> - Site review in approximately 8 weeks
> - Low one-time payment of $99 US
>
> [Basic Submit]
>
> Questions? Visit the <u>Excite Submit FAQ</u> or LookSmart's <u>Customer Service</u>.

- Express Submit: this will take you to a page where you fill out the appropriate information, but again the downside is it costs $199!

- Basic Submit: this costs $99 and takes up to eight weeks to be reviewed.

The forms are the same for both options. Guidelines for submitting can be found at either LookSmart's or Excite's submit page (LookSmart and Excite are partnered websites).

Lycos

Lycos is perhaps the easiest search engine to submit to, just go to home.lycos.com/addasite.html and fill out the short form, but unlike all the other search engines, Lycos offer a "change of address" form! So, in case your website URL changes you can change the index listing! This is a feature which only Lycos seems to be providing.

Before you submit a site, please check whether your URL is already listed on the spider-based catalogue (this does not include the editor-maintained directory).
Enter the complete URL. (e.g. www.lycos.com)

Page URL: `http://`

[Check URL] [Enter new URL]

Submit Site:

Site URL: `http://`

Your e-mail address:
(required)

[Submit URL] [Enter new URL]

Problems?
Please check whether you have entered a correct URL, beginning with "http://www." and ending with a "/" if there is no filename.

Submission Times

Submission timing is also important. Most search engines will only accept a certain number of submissions per day, and after this point any others will be ignored. The best way to avoid this is to submit early in the morning.

Indexing Times

After submitting your site, continue to check frequently whether it has been indexed. The amount of time between your submission and your first appearance on the search engine database can vary, from days to months. If it has not appeared, check the search engine "help" files. This should tell you the right time to submit again. The sections below will give you an idea of indexing times:

Search Engines

altavista
THE SEARCH COMPANY

Probably no more than one month. This is a popular engine and sites are usually indexed quickly and efficiently. If you rank highly with AltaVista your site should receive a lot of visitors.

Inktomi

Usually less than three weeks. However, Inktomi only continue to index pages that have a high enough number of people clicking through into them, so you might have to resubmit after a while.

One way around this is to pay for a listing using www.positiontech.com. This should guarantee a listing in less than five days.

Inktomi powered search engines include All The Web (FAST), AOL, GoTo (shows paid inclusions first), HotBot, LookSmart, and MSN.

excite

This could take some time! It is quite a slow engine; expect to wait about 10 weeks. Some sites are not indexed at all.

Google

This is a very efficient site – you should be indexed in three weeks or less.

Google also operate a reasonably priced listings programme (AdWords), which guarantees that you will be indexed quickly.

Northern Light

on its own

Between two and four weeks. This engine generally responds quickly and is quite competent.

direct hit

Less than two weeks. This is another very responsive search engine.

A long time! Their index is very rarely updated.

As this is a paid service, it is very fast – no more than three days. They also provide other engines with listings, so paying for a top three ranking with GoTo can help you to appear in other engines.

Lycos can be quite slow; it may take up to six weeks.

Directories

YAHOO!

This varies a lot! It could be a matter of days, weeks, months, or even not at all. Yahoo is extremely popular, but is also extremely hard to get listed in.

However, if you really want to be reviewed quickly, they do operate a paid service that guarantees this.

NBCi

Very fast – one week at the most. This is one of the most efficient services available.

dmoz open directory project

About two weeks. This is another first-rate service.

looksmart

This is now run as a paid listing service. Charges vary, but obviously the more you pay, the faster your site will be indexed.

Human Contact

It is a very good idea to try to establish contact with someone working for one of the major search engines. If you can do this, you are a long way towards understanding how the whole system works.

> The best way is to talk to one of the search engines' customer representatives about advertising with them. You will then be assigned a personal account manager who should be able to answer all your questions.

They will then pass you along to hidden pages within their sites, give you contact telephone numbers and email addresses, and will even end up telling you some of their secrets! You will then have secrets that other people do not have, which gives you an edge with the Search Engine Optimisation of your site.

You may even find that the advertisement offers are valuable too. These can include sponsorship and sponsored listings. Sponsorship includes banner advertising on specific pages, whilst sponsored listings give you a top position under a particular keyword or phrase. The costs of advertising vary from engine to engine as does the proposition.

Positiontech

The services offered by Position Technologies (www.positiontech.com) are highly recommended as a way of improving search engine rankings. They offer site analysis for both large and small websites and can help you to optimise your site to your best advantage. They can also guarantee (for an annual subscription fee) your inclusion in the Inktomi index. This is one of the world's leading search services, which includes top engines such as MSN, AOL, HotBot, LookSmart, and many others.

> **HOT TIP** Another advantage is that your site will be indexed within two days.

For as long as your subscription continues, any changes to your website are updated every 48 hours and you receive regular reports on the positions your site has attained.

9

Promotional Methods

Paid Solutions

Sometimes the best things in life aren't always free, sometimes a little money has to change hands to make things happen. Search engines are no different. Like any company they have to make a little money too!

There are three ways that search engines and directories can charge for you to be included within their results…

- Paid Inclusion: This is usually a one-off fee ensuring that your site is within the search engine listings. Sometimes this is the only way to get into a search engine's listings and sometimes it carries fringe benefits beyond those provided by a free inclusion option.

- Paid Placement: This is slightly different from other paid solutions as it can take many forms, from a banner that is returned on a certain keyword enquiry to a highlighted or featured listing which appears at the top of the search engine results.

- Pay-per-Click: Choosing certain keywords and keyword phrases you bid a certain amount per click for each keyword. The rank your site attains in the search results depends on the amount you bid.

These paid solutions are described in more detail in the following sections.

Paid Inclusion

Two of the biggest directories operate a Paid Inclusion service: Yahoo and LookSmart.

The issue to consider with a directory listing such as these is that the submitted sites are guaranteed review by a human editor. Therefore the planning of your submission is very important, and it is imperative you read the submission guidelines on each site.

All commercial listings in Yahoo now have to pay the Yahoo inclusion fee which is $199 (adult sites have to pay $600). This guarantees review, but not inclusion, within 48 hours.

> **HOT TIP:** Yahoo also operate a free listing submission service. This is reserved for non-commercial and regional sites. The review time is significantly slower (eight weeks) and the risk of non-inclusion is greater, but it's free. Most sites, whether commercial or not, have a certain degree of locality. So, when submitting your site to Yahoo, and you want to get in for free, submit to a regional category.

LookSmart, while not providing the traffic that Yahoo does, provides results for many search engines including Excite and AltaVista. So while LookSmart itself may not provide the traffic you crave, its competitors might.

LookSmart charges £149 and promises inclusion within five working days. The most well-documented problem with LookSmart is that the editors actually edit! LookSmart editors edit the title and description of the site and this could leave you right at the bottom of a very large pile!

Not to be outdone the search engines have come up with Paid Inclusion plans. This is true Paid Inclusion, because when you pay, you are included. The advantages of these systems are speedy inclusion time and frequent respidering of your site. While this guarantee does not ensure high placement, it is valuable because with frequent respidering and indexing of your pages you can continue to refine them until they rank highly. Normally, changing them and waiting for the next update would take weeks.

The real pioneers of this system are Inktomi. Inktomi do not provide a search engine themselves: they provide their partners with their database and technology. Inktomi partners include MSN, HotBot and AOL. Several companies provide ways of getting guaranteed inclusion into the Inktomi database. The cheapest is Positiontech (see Chapter 8).

One major search engine has also implemented a Paid Inclusion service: AltaVista. This service, while being almost double the price of Positiontech's, operates in a similar vein (frequent spidering, fast inclusion time). Also the company partnering AltaVista, Infospider, provide a live customer service chat session at www.infospider.com

Paid Placement

Paid Placement is in essence paying for targeted advertising. When purchasing Paid Placement, you are purchasing enhanced exposure on certain searches. The costing model is usually a cost per thousand (CPM) impressions. An impression is simply one showing of your advert or listing.

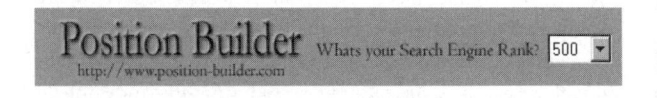

Position Builder Whats your Search Engine Rank? 500
http://www.position-builder.com

One possible method of increasing visitor numbers to your site is banner advertising. Banner ads usually appear on the top of the "results" page after you have done your keyword search, and they are not hard to spot; typically they include moving graphics, bright colours or attention-grabbing headlines. They can also appear in the form of an ordinary application window, (known as a "trick banner") which can fool users into thinking they can click on it without being taken to another web page.

Banner ads are not considered to be the best way of generating traffic to your website as they have a low click-through rate (CTR). It is estimated that for every 500 times that the average banner is shown, only one person will click on it. For this reason, they are generally only used by large and well-established companies who have the time and financial resources to experiment with them.

If you are considering banner advertising for your own website, it might be good to ask yourself a couple of questions first: how often do *you* actually click on banner ads? Also, is the product or service that you offer suited to banner advertising, ie, can it be adequately described in a small space and a few words? If you decide you *do* want to use this as one of your promotional methods, then these are some good rules to follow:

- Experiment first: don't spend huge amounts of money on an all- singing, all-dancing ad campaign, which you later discover is completely ineffective. Start out small and try to determine what works and what doesn't, before moving on to bigger and better things!

- Avoid *too* many fancy graphics: they can distract the user from the main point you are trying to make about your site. They can also take so long to load that by the time they are visible the user has already scrolled down the page. Having said this, it can be a good idea to include a small amount of animation in your ad, as this does tend to attract attention and could improve your CTR.

- Use a "click here" logo in your ad, as this may also help to improve your CTR.

- Stick to the main point: what is your site *really* about? Do you have a unique selling point? Use large, clear lettering and be as concise as possible.

- Target your potential customers: make sure that your ads are in places that are relevant to your own site, so that your intended audience will actually see them. For example, if someone has done a keyword search for vintage cars, it is unlikely that they will click on a banner ad to a site about women's perfume. You may have to pay more to have your ad in all the relevant places, but it will be worth it in the long run.

- Make sure that you direct your click-through visitors to the relevant page. For example, if the banner ad offers a discount on a product, make sure that they are directed to the page dealing with that specific offer. Remember, you don't just want the user to click through, you also want them to hang around and buy your product!

AltaVista offers banner placement on keyword searches. What this means is that when you purchase your impressions for your keyword phrase, your banner will show up when a search for that phrase is performed.

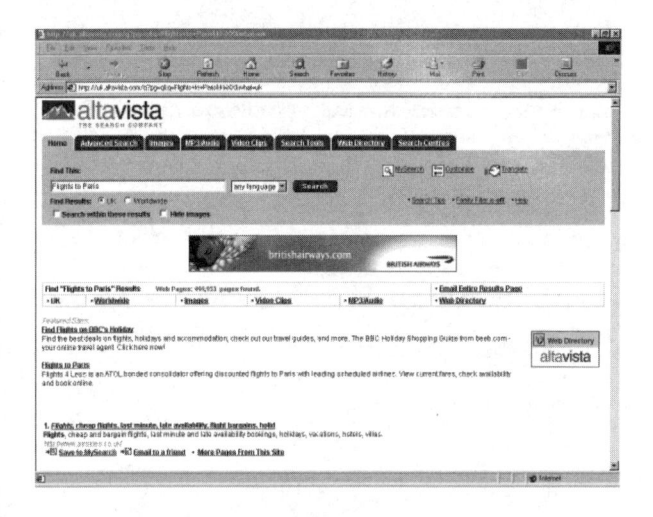

This method of advertising has advantages in the fact that it is very targeted. However, it is very dependent on the choice of keywords and the design of your banner, which of course will influence the number of hits you receive.

Google have their own equivalent in AdWords. This program allows your listing to be placed in a box to the right of all results served on a given keyword search. This is also costed on a CPM basis.

Google's AdWords

Most search engines run a form of advertising on their site, be it banner placement or a featured listing. It is always useful to contact a search engine and discuss the options with a sales representative. This also has the added benefit of providing a personal relationship between yourself and the search engine.

Pay-per-Click   *overture.com*

This is the most complicated but potentially most rewarding type of paid solution available. It is, in theory, as simple as the name would suggest. You do, indeed, pay per click. Every time a user clicks on your listing your account is charged an amount by the search engine. It's the fastest way to drive traffic to your website and the traffic you do receive is highly targeted.

Inclusion in a Pay-per-Click (PPC) engine is essentially free – it starts to cost something when someone clicks on your listing. You simply put down an initial deposit via credit card and then bid on the specific keywords and key phrases that you are interested in. You are then ranked against other companies under each keyword and key phrase, depending on how much you bid for each one. When a user clicks on a link to your website that has been generated from the keyword phrase that you bid on, you are charged whatever that bid was.

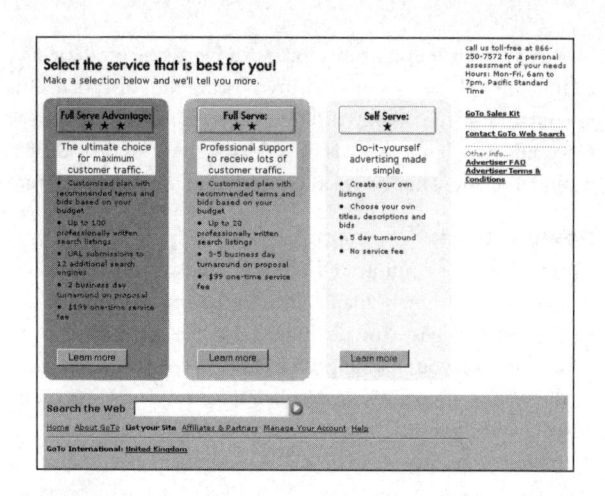

> **HOT TIP:** The main strength of PPC engines is not the actual engines themselves but the fact that most of them feed their listings to other major search engines. For example, if you show up in GoTo's top three bids you'll also show up on the "top ten page" on the same search for the likes of Netscape, AltaVista, Excite, HotBot, AOL Search, DirectHit, etc, and the list seems to grow every day.

Pay-per-Click engines have been criticised in the past for ranking sites according to financial status instead of quality or relevance. The concern is that wealthy companies have the power to buy top positions for any keywords they like, whether related to their site or not. However, Pay-per-Click engines have now recognised the need to provide relevant sites to their customers; they try to ensure that companies cannot buy keywords unless they relate to the site's content. Having said this, it is still true that a high-ranking, relevant site is not necessarily a good quality site.

Pay-per-Click may be a good option for you if you are looking for instant results. Optimising your website could take you some time, and it may be worthwhile to have the extra traffic from paid listings in the meantime. The more popular your keywords are, the more you will need to pay to get a high ranking, so check the bidding prices for your keywords before you go ahead.

When using a PPC engine for your web promotion campaign there are some things to bear in mind…

- Make sure you aren't wasting your money. If you end up paying more for your bid than you are receiving as a result of the clicks, then consider changing keywords or approach.

- Use the tools available to you. Make sure you are selecting the right phrases by using a tool such as Wordtracker, or even GoTo's suggestion tool: inventory.goto.com/d/searchinventory/suggestion/

Suggestion Tool

Not sure what search terms to bid on?
Enter a term related to your site and we will show you:

- Related searches that include your term
- How many times that term was searched on last month

Get suggestions for: (may take up to 30 seconds)

Note: All suggested search terms are subject to our standard editorial review process.

- Grab as many phrases as you can. Try to find out unique phrases and monopolise them. The best thing about finding these well searched, unique phrases is that the top bid will be so small that it's an affordable way of grabbing a sizeable chunk of traffic.

- Check your bids! If you are listed at number 1 for a term that costs 55 pence a click and the number 2 listing is bid at 40 pence per click you are spending extra money on each click needlessly.

- Keep an eye on your referrals. Make sure you are getting relevant traffic. After all you are paying for it.

Link Farms

There are an increasing number of online services offering to submit your site to search engines and directories. These may seem like a good idea, as they are often quite inexpensive and might seem to cut out the hassle of having to submit your site yourself. However, the "search engines" that they submit to are often nothing more than irrelevant lists of sites, which are unlikely to attract potential customers who are specifically looking for the service you offer. Link farms are best avoided – the next section will deal with some better methods of promoting your site.

Link Exchange

A much more reliable method of promoting your website is link exchange. It is always best to exchange links with companies that are similar to your own; this way you can be sure that those who see your link are already specifically looking for your type of service. The first thing to do is to locate a number of companies that are similar to your own. To find these, use a directory (such as Yahoo) to do a search under your own keywords. Choose some of the sites listed and send them a polite letter or email explaining who you are and outlining the benefits of link exchange.

HOT TIP: Try to make your emails personal to each individual company rather than sending out a general letter. This may take more time, but it will improve the chances of your email being read rather than being rejected as spam.

DON'T FORGET: No matter which of these methods you use, it is still true that the best way to promote your Internet business is to develop a good quality website; you will probably find that if you do this, others will link to you without even being asked.

If you have followed this guide through so far and your site has gained a high position, you will want it to stay there! In the next chapter you will learn about the steps you need to take to keep your site at the top…

10

Conclusion

Your Work's Not Over Yet!

Okay, so you have worked through this guide step by step. You have spent hours painstakingly optimising your website. All your hard work has finally paid off; your search engine rankings have improved dramatically. Now what? Well, you may be tempted to simply breathe a sigh of relief, put your feet up and enjoy reaping the benefits of your new-found web position, never again having to delve into the complicated world of search engine optimisation…

Sorry to break it to you, but as with most things in life that are worth doing, it is not as easy as all that! Once your site is listed highly, chances are you will want it to stay there, and this takes (yes, you guessed it) a little more work. Search engine rankings change constantly, for all kinds of reasons. Search engines review their indexes regularly, adding new sites, updating some, and dropping others. To stay on top, you may need to make regular changes to your site, depending on the changes in your ranking.

Monitoring and Maintaining Your Position

There are a number of ways in which you can monitor the progress of your website after it has been submitted to the search engines. Firstly, make sure your site has definitely been listed – you won't get very far if it hasn't, and as you saw earlier, getting indexed is not always as easy as you may imagine. To check this, type in your domain name and see if your site comes up.

Secondly, you need to check your ranking in each search engine you have submitted to, and there are a number of ways to do this. You can do it yourself by typing in your keyword phrases one by one in each engine. However, this could be time consuming, particularly for larger businesses with a lot of keywords for each different product or service. You may prefer to use one of the many online services that will tell you the position your site has attained across the engines, for example, Market Position (www.marketposition.com) or Gogettem (www.gogettem.com).

Once you have checked your rankings, you will need to make regular changes to keep the positions you have attained. You can do this yourself using the tips given in this guide, or alternatively you can use an online service that will do the work for you in return for a fee. There are several highly recommended optimisation services. Position Builder (www.position-builder.com) will secure your site a position within the top 20 search results. They are experienced optimisation specialists and can also offer advice and support on all technical issues relating to search engineering. Positiontech (www.positiontech.com) also offer advice and support, and can advise you of the changes necessary to optimise your site. (Chapter 8 gives more information on Positiontech.)

Once you have checked your position, you may want to make some changes before resubmitting your site to the engines. There is really no need to resubmit if you are already ranking highly, although many people do choose to do this regularly anyway to ensure that they stay indexed.

> As a general rule, if your site is ranking well and you are happy with the amount of traffic it receives, don't change it – you could even damage your site's ranking if you do.

Java Code

If the success of your online business depends upon you ranking highly, it is best to avoid the use of JavaScript pages as much as possible. There are technical reasons for this, but basically, sites that have a lot of Java tend to rank lower than those that don't, so try to avoid it if possible.

Dynamically Generated Pages

If your website includes dynamically generated web pages, you will probably experience difficulties in being indexed by search engine spiders. This is because dynamic sites include a question mark in their URL, which throws spiders into confusion when they are attempting to "crawl" through your site's content. As a result, they stop crawling, and therefore your site is not indexed. "Static" web pages (those without meta refresh tags, cloaking, or similar techniques) are indexed easily. However, if you only have one or two static pages (which are indexed), the engines will probably not consider your site to be content-rich enough to be included in their listings. Getting around this problem is not easy; most people opt for professional help from search engine specialists, such as those mentioned earlier, to help them get their pages indexed. It does not appear that search engines are going to change their rules for dynamic sites in the near future.

Glossary

Agent Name Delivery
When a particular search engine's spider comes to index your site, the spider identifies itself by its user agent string. If the string is recognised, the engine will automatically be served with the page you have specifically optimised for it.

Cascading Style Sheets
Cascading Style Sheets (CSS) are used to add simple display styles to web pages.

CGI
An acronym for Common Gateway Interface. CGI refers to programs that are used to produce on-the-fly content for browser delivery. Common CGI programming languages include Perl, C, and PHP.

Cloaking
Using some system to hide code content from a user, and deliver custom content to a search engine spider.

Directory

A directory is a website that focuses on listing websites by individual topics. It is like a table of contents. A search engine lists pages, whereas a directory (such as LookSmart or Open Directory) lists websites.

Doorway Page

A page designed as an entrance to a website. Many Doorway pages are specifically created to rank high on a particular search engine. Sometimes referred to as a Strategic Entry Point.

Filter Words

This term is often confused with Stop words. Filter words are common words that search engines remove from web pages before adding the pages to their databases. These include words along the lines of "the", "is", "an", "of", "for", "do". As you can imagine, removing these words can save search engines enormous amounts of database space.

See also: Stop Words

Frames

An HTML tag construct for making a website appear to have multiple windows within one browser. A frame with links can remain static while clicks cause a different frame to be updated. Most serious websites stay away from frame usage because of browser compatibility problems and search engine problems. Most search engines will not index a framed site.

Gateway Page

A page containing a list of links to all the pages of your website. Gateway pages do not need to rank highly within the search engines, but when a spider finds your Gateway page, it *should* follow all the links to your site. The advantage of this is that some search engines give higher rankings to pages the spider finds itself.

HTML

HyperText Markup Language. The programming language of tag commands used in web pages.

Image Map

A system of associating parts of an image with hyperlinks. For example a picture of the earth could have hyperlinks associated with various locations. Selecting a particular location might take you to information about that location.

Inbound Link

A link pointing to a website. When a user arrives at a website from another site, that link is called an Inbound Link.

Indexer

When a search engine spiders, or downloads, a page on a website, it must process the page to store it. A spider is responsible for the downloading, while the indexer is responsible for processing the page. A search engine indexer will typically process a page by removing all HTML tags, checking for story links, often compressing the page by pulling out Filter words, looking for Stop words, and finally storing the page in an online searchable database.

Inktomi

A search engine database of sites that just services other search engines providing search results. Inktomi provides more searches per search engine than any other site on the Internet. Some of its bigger partners are HotBot, MSN, GoTo and AOL Netfind.

Invisible Text

Placing characters of a certain colour on the same colour background causes them to be hidden. This technique was popular for a while, but search engines quickly caught on and began banning sites for it.

IP Address

Whenever you connect to the Internet, you are giving a unique four-number Internet Protocol address (IP address). Your IP address is how data finds its way back and forth between your computer and a website.

Your IP address may change each time you attach to your ISP. If your IP address stays the same from connection to connection, you are said to have a static IP address. If it changes each time you connect, you are said to have a dynamic IP address.

IP addresses can be important in the context of search engine submission because some search engines have been known to ignore submissions from any IP address over a certain limit.

IP Delivery

Refers to the process of delivering customised content based upon the user's IP address. This allows websites to protect their proprietary code designed to rank high on search engines.

JavaScript

A language embedded within HTML that is executed after a page of HTML is transferred to a user's browser. Many search engines will ignore Java and JavaScript commands.

Keyword

A single word or phrase that is typed into a search engine search query. Keyword mainly refers to popular words which relate to any one website. For example, a website about real estate could focus on keywords such as "House", or phrases such as "Home for Sale".

Keyword Density

A percentage measure of how many times a keyword is repeated within the text of a page. For example, if a page contains 100 words and 10 of those words are "house", then "house" is said to have a 10% keyword density. There are programs that will rate keyword density by single words or by groups of words, for example, "new home for sale".

Keyword Stuffing

The process of loading a page up with keywords in the Meta Tags or main HTML body.

Link Popularity

A count of the number of links pointing at a website (Inbound Links). Many search engines now count link popularity in their algorithms.

Meta Tag

Author-generated HTML commands that are placed in the head section of an HTML document. Current popular Meta Tags that can affect search engine rankings are keywords and descriptions.

The keywords Meta Tag is used to group a series of words that relate to a website. These tags can be used by search engines to classify pages for searches.

The descriptions Meta Tag is used to describe the document. The description is then displayed in search engine results.

The robots Meta Tag is used to control certain aspects of how a search engine indexes the page.

An HTTP-EQUIV Meta Tag can sometimes be used to issue some server HTTP commands. Most common is an HTTP REFRESH command. Gaining in popularity is a NOCACHE command to thwart server caching of a page.

Other useful tags are the CHAR SET tag to describe the document language and character set, the author Meta Tag and the generator Meta Tag (software used to generate the page).

Multiple Submission

Term used for a web user continually submitting their website in the hope that the spider will visit their site quicker.

PPC

Pay-per-Click. A Pay-per-Click search engine charges websites on a per click basis. Often, an auction is held to see who is willing to pay the most for specific keywords.

Robot

A program that automatically does some action without user intervention. In the context of search engines, it usually refers to a program that mimics a browser to download web pages automatically. A spider is a type of robot. Robots are sometimes referred to as webbots.

See also: Spider

robots.txt

A file in the root directory of a website that is used to control which spiders have access to which pages within the website. When a spider or robot connects to a website, it checks for the presence of a robots.txt file. Only spiders that adhere to the Robots Exclusion Standard will obey a robots.txt command file.

There are several specific fields in a robots.txt file, such as "User-agent" which specifies which user agents are allowed to access the site, and "Allow" and "Disallow" which specify which directories a spider may access.

Search Engine

A search engine is a computer-operated database of web pages. When you search for something on the Internet, you submit keywords to a search engine. It then returns a list of all the web pages containing the keywords you typed in.

SEO

Search Engine Optimisation. This refers to the process of optimising your website so that it achieves a high position in search engine listings. This in turn will increase the website's exposure to potential customers.

Spam

The submission of pages that are intended to rank artificially high by various unethical techniques. This can include submitting hundreds of slightly different pages designed to rank high; pages containing small, invisible text; or word-scrambled pages. Most of these techniques are flagged by search engines as spam.

Spider

The main program used by search engines to retrieve web pages for inclusion in their database.

See also: Robot

Stemming

Refers to word roots. For example, "Search", "Searching", and "Searches" all have "Search" as the root or stem. Some search engines use stemming to provide results from more than just the entered search terms, so that a search on "Boat" could return results on "Boating" or "Boats".

Stop Words

This term has been so often confused with Filter words that it now refers to Filter words most of the time. A Stop word is a word that causes an indexer to STOP indexing in the current procedure and do something else. Most commonly, this is when an indexer encounters an adult or censored word.

See also: Filter Words

Submission

The act of submitting a web page to a search engine or submitting a website to a directory.

URL

Universal Resource Locator. The basis of how we find websites on the Internet. URLs can include different forms of communicating with a server: an HTTP URL is HyperText Transfer Protocol while an FTP URL is a File Transfer Protocol. You can determine how you are connecting with a site by looking at the beginning of a URL for the HTTP, FTP, or other protocol identifier. Most websites are located on HTTP servers and begin with "http://".

In the context of search engines, URLs are important because they contain entities which the search engine may or may not like. For example, your domain may include keywords related to your website.

User Agent

Each time a web browser or other client connects to a website, they report a USER_AGENT. Common user agents include Netscape, Opera, and Internet Explorer. In the context of search engine robots or spiders, a CGI program can read the USER_AGENT and deliver custom content to that user or robot. The user agent can also be included in a robots.txt file to allow or deny access to the website.

Index

A

Absolute links 37
AdWords 96
Agent name delivery 46
All The Web 54, 72
ALT text 22, 65
AltaVista 51, 70, 82, 92, 95
AOL 52
ASCII 39
Ask Jeeves 53
ASP. *See* Dynamically generated pages

B

BackRub 73
Banners 92
Blank cells 24
Body content 21, 63

C

Cascading style sheets 41
CGI 46
Click-through rate 93
Cloaking 45
Cold Fusion. *See* Dynamically generated pages
Commas 19
Comments 40, 65
Competition 12
Competitor analysis 12
Cost per thousand 92
CPM 92
Crawling 61
CSS 41
CTR 93

D

Description Meta Tag 17, 64
Design, of website 15
Direct Hit 53, 66, 84
Directory 3

dmoz. See Open Directory
Doorways 29, 41
Dynamically generated pages 106

E

Excite 54, 79, 83
Existing customers 10

F

FAST 54
Filter words 9
Flash 28
Frames 25, 61
Frameset 25

G

Gateways 30
Generating keywords 10
Gogettem 104
Google 55, 73, 84, 96
GoogleBot 73
GoTo 55, 85
    Suggestion tool 99

H

Header tags 24
Hidden form fields 50
Hidden links 38
Hidden text 37, 68
HotBot 56, 75
HTML 2, 16, 32, 40, 50

I

Images 22
Indexing 2, 63
Indexing times 82
InfoSpider 71, 92
Inktomi 57, 83
Invisible pixels 36
Invisible text. See Hidden text
IP address delivery 46

J

Java 106
JavaScript 44, 106
JSP. See Dynamically generated pages

K

Keyword density 14
Keyword phrases 9
Keyword stuffing 21
Keyword weighting 13
Keywords 5
Keywords Meta Tag 17, 64

L

Law and keywords 20
Link exchange 101
Link farms 33, 101
Link popularity 33, 62, 66
Links 23
LookSmart 57, 78, 86, 90
Lycos 58, 81, 85

M

Magellan 54
Market Position 34, 104
Meta refresh 44, 67
Meta Tags 17, 66
Misspellings 8
Monitoring your position 104
MSN 58

N

NBCi 59, 86
Netscape 60
Netscape Search 55, 56
No Frames tag 27
Northern Light 59, 84

O

Open Directory 60, 76, 86

P

Paid Inclusion 63, 89, 90
Paid Placement 90, 92
Pay-per-Click 90, 97
Planning for each search engine 35
Position Builder 105
Positiontech 88, 105
Potential customers 10
Presto chango 48

R

Ranking 65
Referrals 101
Revisits 63
Robot 2
Robot handling 46
Robots Meta Tag 32, 62
robots.txt 47

S

Scooter 46
Search engine 2
Search engine optimisation 3

Slurp 46
Snap 59
Spam 21, 49, 66
Spider 2
Stop words 9, 63
Submission, manual 69
Submission times 82

T

Tables 23
Text formatting 24
Title 16

W

WebCrawler 54, 85
Wired Digital 56
Wordtracker 7, 99
World Wide Web Worm 56

Y

Yahoo 60, 74, 86, 90